HAL•LEONARD
INSTRUMENTAL
PLAY-ALONG

AUDIO
ACCESS
INCLUDED

PLAYBACK+
Speed • Pitch • Balance • Loop

HORN

12 HOT SINGLES

Audio arrangements by Peter Deneff

To access audio visit:
**www.halleonard.com/mylibrary**
Enter Code
4833-0455-8699-6668

ISBN 978-1-5400-5893-5

HAL•LEONARD®

Visit Hal Leonard Online at
**www.halleonard.com**

Contact us:
**Hal Leonard**
7777 West Bluemound Road
Milwaukee, WI 53213
Email: info@halleonard.com

In Europe, contact:
**Hal Leonard Europe Limited**
42 Wigmore Street
Marylebone, London, W1U 2RN
Email: info@halleonardeurope.com

In Australia, contact:
**Hal Leonard Australia Pty. Ltd.**
4 Lentara Court
Cheltenham, Victoria, 3192 Australia
Email: info@halleonard.com.au

# CONTENTS

# BROKEN

HORN

Words and Music by MITCHELL COLLINS,
CHRISTIAN MEDICE and SAMANTHA DeROSA

# THE MIDDLE

Horn

Words and Music by SARAH AARONS,
MARCUS LOMAX, JORDAN JOHNSON,
ANTON ZASLAVSKI, KYLE TREWARTHA,
MICHAEL TREWARTHA and STEFAN JOHNSON

# HAVANA

Horn

Words and Music by CAMILA CABELLO, LOUIS BELL,
PHARRELL WILLIAMS, ADAM FEENEY, ALI TAMPOSI,
JEFFERY LAMAR WILLIAMS, BRIAN LEE, ANDREW WOTMAN,
BRITTANY HAZZARD and KAAN GUNESBERK

# HEAVEN

Horn

Words and Music by SHY CARTER,
LINDSAY RIMES and MATTHEW McGINN

# HIGH HOPES

Horn

Words and Music by BRENDON URIE,
SAMUEL HOLLANDER, WILLIAM LOBBAN BEAN,
JONAS JEBERG, JACOB SINCLAIR,
JENNY OWEN YOUNGS, ILSEY JUBER,
LAUREN PRITCHARD and TAYLOR PARKS

# NATURAL

Horn

Words and Music by DAN REYNOLDS,
WAYNE SERMON, BEN McKEE,
DANIEL PLATZMAN, JUSTIN TRANTOR,
MATTIAS LARSSON and ROBIN FREDRICKSSON

# NO PLACE LIKE YOU

Horn

Words and Music by TROY VERGES,
BRETT JAMES and JOSHUA MILLER

# SHALLOW

## from A STAR IS BORN

Horn

Words and Music by STEFANI GERMANOTTA,
MARK RONSON, ANDREW WYATT
and ANTHONY ROSSOMANDO

# SUCKER

Horn

Words and Music by NICK JONAS,
JOSEPH JONAS, CARL ROSEN,
RYAN TEDDER, LOUIS BELL,
ADAM FEENEY and KEVIN JONAS

# SUNFLOWER

from SPIDER-MAN: INTO THE SPIDER-VERSE

Horn

Words and Music by AUSTIN RICHARD POST,
CARL AUSTIN ROSEN, KHALIF BROWN,
CARTER LANG, LOUIS BELL
and BILLY WALSH

# YOUNGBLOOD

Horn

Words and Music by ASHTON IRWIN,
CALUM HOOD, LOUIS BELL,
LUKE HEMMING, ALEXANDRA TAMPOSI
and ANDREW WATT

To Coda ⊕

# THANK U, NEXT

HORN

Words and Music by ARIANA GRANDE,
VICTORIA McCANTS, KIMBERLY KRYSIUK,
TAYLA PARX, TOMMY BROWN,
CHARLES ANDERSON and MICHAEL FOSTER